Place Value Mysteries

US 101

by B. A. Shaver

STECK-VAUGHN

Harcourt Supplemental Publishers

www.steck-vaughn.com

Here is a number mystery for you to solve.
How many people do you think are in this photo?

Hundreds	Tens	Ones

1 hundred, *8 tens,* **and** 7 ones **make** 187 sheep.

Here is another number mystery.
Many tulips are growing in this field.
How many tulips are there?
Read the clues to solve the number mystery.

Clues

Here are the number clues.

- The number of tulips is more than 200.
- The number of tulips is less than 600.
- The number of tulips has a 5 in the hundreds place.
- The number of tulips has a 1 in the ones place.

351   135   531

Which is the mystery number?

If you guessed (531) tulips, then you solved the mystery!

Clues

- The number (531) is more than 200.

- The number (531) is less than 600.

- The number (531) has a 5 in the hundreds place.

- The number (531) has a 1 in the ones place.

Hundreds	Tens	Ones

5 hundreds, 3 tens, and 1 one make 531 tulips.

Here is another number mystery.
This table is covered with pennies.
How many pennies are on this table?
Read the clues to solve the number mystery.

Clues

Here are the number clues.
- The number of pennies is more than 700.
- The number of pennies is less than 900.
- The number of pennies has an 8 in the tens place.
- The number of pennies has a 2 in the ones place.

782 — 872 — 282

Which is the mystery number?

If you guessed (782) pennies, then you solved the mystery!

Clues

- The number (782) is more than 700.

- The number (782) is less than 900.

- The number (782) has an 8 in the tens place.

- The number (782) has a 2 in the ones place.

Hundreds	Tens	Ones

7 hundreds, 8 tens, and 2 ones make 782 pennies.

There are 19 fish swimming in the ocean.
How many tens are in the number 19?
How many ones are there?
What other clues could you give about the number 19?
Try making a place value mystery of your own!